NINJA QUEENi

Kelly Clegg

TABLE OF CONTENTS

Introduction 1

Quick Start Reference 4

Tinned Roast Potatoes 5

Air Crisp Chips 6

Roasted Chickpeas 7

Root Vegetable Soup 8

Beef Stew 9

Creamy Mash Potatoes 10

Celery Chicken 11

Chicken Curry in a Hurry 12

Lemon & Herb Roast Chicken 13

Jacket Potatoes 14

Cider Pork Casserole 15

Speedy Vegetable Risotto 16

Honey Glazed Gammon 17

Pork Leg (with crackling) 18

Doner Kebab 19

Pasta Bolognese 20

Rice Pudding 21

Fluffy White Rice 22

Sausage Rolls 23

Sriracha & Honey Salmon	24
Tandoori Drumsticks	25
Tomato Risotto	26
Chicken Wings	27
Krispy Kale	28
Biscoff Brownies	29
Cheese Scones	30
Pasta Arrabiata	31
Mulled Wine	32
Flapjacks	33
Green Thai Curry	34
Hot Chocolate	35
Cleggys Chilli	36
Air Crisp Tortillas	37
Halloumi Omelette	38
Spanish Chicken	39
Chickpea Curry	40
Fish Pie	41
Camembert Dippers	43
Strawberry Jam	44
Pizza Swirls	45
Sweet Potato Fries	46
Cauliflower Cheese	47
Fruit Cake	48
Cheese Toastie	49

Fried Chicken 50

Potato Skins 51

Chicken And Chorizo Paella 52

Roast Veg Tray Bake 53

Stuffed Mushrooms 54

Dumpling Soup 55

INTRODUCTION

This cookbook is for anyone who is starting out with the Ninja Foodi or anyone looking for inspiration on what to try next. I am a busy full time working mum from the uk , so time, easily available ingredients, and tasty fresh food is really important to me. You probably have most of the ingredients mentioned in this book in your cupboards and fridge already, by utilising your Ninja Foodi to cook your favourite home cooked meals, I hope you will find that you save time and it takes a little stress out of cooking or even thinking what's for dinner.

The recipes are completely straightforward and easy to follow while getting the best out of your Ninja. You will find, like any recipe, that there are more ways than one to cook your meal and it is finding the best way for YOU. All these recipes are completely adaptable to suit your needs. These are everyday meals and snacks because i believe if the food is too fancy and difficult to make, you just won't end up cooking it.

As a mum it's really important to me that my family eat healthy home cooked food but some days time is against me and i feel guilty for ordering a takeaway, but since i got the multicooker it is quicker for me to cook something myself rather than wait for a delivery, making the Ninja Foodi a healthy way of eating as you will find not a lot of oil is required and you can add as much veg as you like. I use spray olive oil, but you can use what suits you. Of course, it doesn't all HAVE to be healthy, you can bake cakes ect in your ninja too, it's all about balance.

I hate food waste and love getting my 5 a day so don't be afraid to add in extra or substitutes, whatever works for you. The multicooker is a wonderful time saver but at first it can be intimidating and i want to show you how to get the most out of it.

Okay let's get started with the basics and how the Ninja Foodi actually works.

- **Pressure cook (PC):** Use to cook food quickly while maintaining tenderness. You might find with meat and poultry to use this function to cook then air crisp or roast to make it crispy.

Water for Pressure-Cooking: pressure-cooking needs steam to do its job, and some form of liquid starts this process. Always ensure you add at minimum of half a cup of water to the inside pot before pressure cooking foods to make your cooking successful. This can be stock for example. Always read and follow the manufacturer's instructions and I recommend you do the water test first to get the hang of it. The ninja will tell you if you need to add more water.

Water test: Place the inside bowl into the Ninjai, Add 3 cups of room-temp water to the pot, Now shut the Ninja Foodi by placing a pressure lid on, Following the arrow on the lid with an arrow on the front of the Ninja cooker base. Now turn the pressure lid clockwise; the lid will lock into place.Turn the release valve to the seal position on the pressure lid. Click the pressure button on the control panel, the Ninja Foodi will automatically default to high pressure with the timer setting itself 2 minutes. Then click the START/STOP button to activate. The Ninja Foodi will start to build pressure inside the unit, with the rotating lights indicating the unit is building up pressure (around 5-10 mins). Once fully pressurized, the Ninja will start counting down 2 minutes. When the 2-minute countdown is complete, the Ninja Foodi will make a beeping sound, switch itself to the Keep Warm mode automatically, then it will begin counting up (this is called natural release). You can quickly release the pressurized steam by switching the pressure release valve to the VENT position (use a wooden spoon to do this the first time as it's quite loud!). A fast blast of steam will flow out of the pressure release valve. After the steam is totally released, the Ninja Foodi is ready to open.

- **Steam:** Use to gently cook delicate foods, such as fish or vegetables at high temperatures
- **Slow cook:** Cooks food like soup or stews at a lower temperature for longer periods (preheat the bowl first on saute before slow cooking)
- **Sear/saute:** The same as using a hot pan for browning meats, sauteing vegetables or simmering sauces, fabulous for stir frys or thickening after pressure cooking

- **Air crisp:** This is the Ninja Foodi as an air fryer meaning you can cook things like fries using only a small amount of oil (for frozen chips i don't add any further oil)
- **Bake/roast:** This is the setting to use to roast meat or make bread, cakes and other baked items
- **Lids:** You have two lids, the **Air Crisping Lid** for air frying and the **Pressure Lid** for pressure-cooking. Make proper use of each lid as instructed by the recipe you are using at the time. When you aren't using the pressure lid, please ensure you store it safely. You could put a hoot on a wall or inside a cupboard for storage.
- **Always Use the Inside Pot/bowl:** The Ninja tells you if the inside pot isn't in before cooking. Before adding anything to your Ninja PLEASE ensure the pot/bowl is in place. If you use any other accessories, the pot still needs to be in there first. I use wooden and plastic spoons/stirrers etc to protect the bowl. You can buy extra accessories for your ninja for baking etc.
- **Keep Warm:** This automatically turns on after steaming, slow cooking, or pressure-cooking time is done. Ninja Foodi is made to keep this mode on for up to 12 hours if you don't switch it off
- **Power button:** Don't forget to power off when you have finished!
- **Start / Stop button**: Use to start and stop!
- **Temp buttons**: Up and down buttons to select your temperature
- **Cleaning**: NEVER place the Ninja Foodi base immersed in water or put in the dishwasher. When cleaning the Ninja Foodi base and control panel, just wipe clean with a damp (not wet) cloth. The inside cooking pot/bowl, reversible rack, detachable diffuser, Cook & Crisp Basket, and silicone ring can be washed with a dishwasher. Always ensure the cooking pot/bowl is completely dry, especially the outside before placing back inside the Ninja. The pressure lid, anti-clog cap, and pressure release valve can be cleaned with water and mild detergent. NEVER clean the pressure lid or its parts in the dishwasher, and DO NOT take apart the red float valve assembly or pressure release valve. Be gentle, no harsh chemical or scrubbing.

QUICK START REFERENCE

AIR CRISP

FRIES 200c 15mins

BACON 200c 8mins

BROCCOLI 200c 8mins

SAUSAGES 200c 15mins

SALMON FILLETS 180c 10mins

CHICKEN FILLETS 190c 20mins

PRESSURE COOK

BROCCOLI- Half a cup of water, 1 min on low, quick release

BRUSSEL SPROUTS- (cut in half) Half a cup of water, 1 min on low, quick release

BONELESS CHICKEN BREAST 2LB- 1 cup of water, 8-10mins on high, quick release

CAULIFLOWER- Half a cup of water, 1 min on low, quick release

BASMATI RICE- 1 cup of rice needs 1 cup of water, 2 mins on high, natural release 10 mins then quick release

STEAM

BROCCOLI CHOPPED - 5mins

CAULIFLOWER- 5-6mins

PEAS- 3mins

BRUSSEL SPROUTS- 8-10mins

SMALL POTATO CUBES- 15-20mins

CARROTS (SLICED)0 6-8mins

TINNED ROAST POTATOES

This is a super easy, quick, cheap and tasty recipe to get you started and can accompany almost anything. You don't even have to do any chopping or peeling for these tasty spuds. It's a great way to get started and you can also add any fresh herbs you might have.

All you need:

A Tin of Potatoes
Salt, Pepper and Garlic powder
Spray oil

Method:

- Open the tin of potatoes and drain
- Put them into your bowl and add salt, pepper and garlic salt (or any other herbs or seasonings that take your fancy) and spray with oil
- Air crisp for 20 mins at 200

AIR CRISP CHIPS

Everyone's favourite and by using the air crisp function it makes these chips a healthier option to have with almost anything. Chips are probably one of the first things people want to make in an air fryer and something you will make again and again. Add chopped chilli, spring onions and grated cheese for the last 2 mins to make them into dirty fries.

All you need:

Potatoes
Spray oil
Salt and Pepper (and any other seasoning you'd like to add)

Method:

- Peel and cut potatoes
- Leave in salt water for 30 mins (this takes out the starch, skip this part if in a hurry
- Pat the potatoes down with a towel to dry
- Spray with oil and add any seasoning you desire (if any) salt, pepper, paprika, garlic powder, Cajun spice to name a few
- Air crisp for 30 mins at 180

ROASTED CHICKPEAS

I LOVE these! These make a great alternative to peanuts and are full of fibre and protein. The bonus is they are super easy to make. I think everyone has a can of chickpeas in the back of the cupboard and these are the perfect savoury snack to enjoy with a movie. I like to store mine in the mason jar and label it with the different flavours. They go down a treat at Christmas time for table snacks in different flavours.

All you need:

A tin of Chickpeas

Seasoning's- such as salt & pepper, garlic salt, chilli powder, curry powder, cajun seasoning. BBQ etc

Method:

- Drain the chickpeas
- add your flavourings
- 16 mins on air crisp at 200

TIP: The water from the chickpeas (Aquafaba) is used as an egg substitute. You can mix 100ml of Aquafaba with 110g of caster sugar to make vegan meringues or use for other dairy free recipes!

ROOT VEGETABLE SOUP

This soup is so simple to make and a delicious winter warmer. It's full of yummy nutritious vegetables and is ideal to put in the freezer or in a flask to take to work or go on a walk. If you have any leftover chicken you can shred it and add it in or add a spoonful of cream at the end to make it creamy. I don't like waste so if you have any vegetables in the fridge that have seen better days, don't be afraid to add it in and use it all up. You can also freeze the soup if you make too much and have it another day.

All you need:

You can buy a pack of fresh ready chopped root veg at your local supermarket for ease or alternately-

2 onions	*1 potato*	*Two garlic cloves*
1 leek	*1 turnip*	*Salt & pepper*
3 carrots	*Vegetable stock cube*	*Fresh coriander to serve*

Method:

- Peel & chop all vegetable
- Add the stock cube with 500 ml of boiling water (or as directed)
- Add garlic salt and salt & pepper
- Pressure cook on high for 20 mins
- You can eat the soup like this or alternatively blend with a blender to make it thick and smooth. Add chopped fresh coriander to serve.

BEEF STEW

You can't go wrong with this hearty and tasty beef stew. Full of goodness and flavour this recipe is always a winner for the full family and I always seem empty plates when serving this dish. It goes perfectly with creamy mash. Again, if you have any other vegetables going spare then add them in and you can swap the beef with chicken and use chicken stock.

All you need:

Braising steak/ stewing beef diced, 500g

2 cloves of Garlic

2 Onions

4 Carrots

2 Potatoes

Chestnut mushrooms 180g

Red lentils

Beef stock cube

Method:

- Peel and chop all the vegetables
- Add the vegetables, lentils and beef into the pot and enough beef stock to ensure all the food is covered
- Pressure cook for 35 mins on high. Served with mash and freeze any leftovers

TIP: You can spray oil and put the beef in first and set to saute to first to brown the meat if you prefer. Then add everything in.

CREAMY MASH POTATOES

Perfect to serve with beef stew and almost anything really! You can add some grated cheddar or mozzarella to make cheesy mash, which is out of this world!

All you need:

Potatoes (baking potatoes or Maris pipers)
Butter
Milk
Salt & pepper

Method:

- Peel and chop potatoes
- Add 600 ml of water, pressure cook on high for 10 mins
- Transfer out of the ninja for mashing
- Add two knobs of butter and a splash of milk and mash the potatoes
- Add cheese if you desire

CELERY CHICKEN

My son loves this recipe and goes perfectly with rice or green sautéed vegetables or even on its own with some garlic bread. It's a recipe for all seasons.

All you need:

Chicken Breast (one for each person you are cooking for)	3 batons of celery	2 Onions
	Red pepper	1 large Potato
	10 Cherry tomatoes	Chicken stock

Method:

- Cop the celery, red pepper, onions and potato
- Cut the cherry tomatoes in half and add all veg and the chicken to the ninja pot
- Add the chicken stock 500 ml (enough to cover ingredients)
- Pressure cook for 25 mins on high

CHICKEN CURRY IN A HURRY

Why would you order a Saturday night takeaway when you can cook a delicious, healthy curry in less than an hour?! Since I got my ninja, takeaways are a thing of the past because it's quicker, cheaper and easier to make the food myself. This curry in a hurry is super tasty and can be enjoyed with rice and naan bread. It's a firm family favourite and you can swap the chicken for chickpeas, beef, prawns or fish.

All you need:

- Chicken, diced (or alternative)
- 2 cloves of Garlic
- Grated ginger around 4cm
- Tin of chopped Tomatoes
- 1 large Onion
- 2 handfuls of Spinach
- 2 teaspoons of Garam masala
- 1 teaspoon Curry powder
- 1 teaspoon ground cumin
- 1 teaspoon of Tomato puree
- 1 red Chilli

Method:

- Peel and chop onion & garlic
- Grate the ginger
- Add all ingredients to the ninja bowl and stir in
- Cook on pressure cooker high 25 mins

LEMON & HERB ROAST CHICKEN

I don't wait for Sunday to have a roast, this mouth watering chicken is perfect for any day of the week and is enjoyed by the whole family. I sometimes serve with salad, home-made coleslaw and tortilla wraps and other times with roast potatoes and vegetables. You can even put your roast potatoes in with the chicken on the air crisp setting making this teatime treat super easy and simple. You can easily adapt the seasoning and flavours for your chicken, for example you can use the tandoori recipe for this but still use this cooking method. You can also roast a chicken using the air crisp function only, but i find this method here results in a juicy chicken.

All you need:

Chicken (medium)
3 Garlic cloves, roughly chopped
Mixed herbs
Lemon
Spray oil
Chicken stock 1 litre (there is a liquid measure inside the bowl to help you)

Method:

- Mixed the juice of a lemon, mixed herbs, garlic and oil in a small bowl
- Rub generously into the chicken (under the skin, into the nooks)
- Add the made up chicken stock to the pot
- Pressure cook for 20 mins
- After pressure cooking is finished (it doesn't look very appealing at this stage but don't worry). Remove the liquid from the pot, I use a ladle to scope the stock out and put it in a jug for later use for soup/gravy etc
- Air crisp for 20 mins on high

TIP: Depending on the size of your chicken you may want to cook a little longer. You can purchase a meat thermometer to check the internal temperature of the meat. The pressure cook basically cooks the chicken, while the air crisp function gets it nice and crispy.

JACKET POTATOES

My bonfire night fave! For the perfect jacket potatoes that are fluffy in the middle and crispy on the outside.

All you need:

Jacket potatoes
Spray oil
Salt & pepper

Method:

- Prick the potatoes with a fork
- Add the potatoes to the pot with 250 ml of water
- Pressure cook high for 15 mins and quick release
- Drain the water and pat dry the potatoes
- Spray with oil and season with salt & pepper and roast for 15 mins
- Air crisp 15 mins

CIDER PORK CASSEROLE

This is one of my favourite Sunday meals, I put this in the slow cooker while I clean the house and take the dog for a long walk. By the time I've finished for the day this pork casserole smells beautiful and is ready to eat! I enjoy it with some crusty bread and butter or rice if I am trying to be good!

All you need:

500g diced Pork
Fresh parsley
1 Stick of celery
1 Onion

15 Button mushrooms
2 Carrots
250 ml dry Cider
60 ml double Cream

Spray oil
Salt & pepper
Vegetable stock

Method:

- Spray the oil into the ninja bowl and put the ninja on sauté mode ,brown the diced pork- no need to fully cook. Once browned, switch this mode off
- Add chopped carrots, celery, carrots and you can add the button mushrooms whole to the pork
- Add 250ml of veg stock and the cider to the pot
- Add salt & pepper and give it a good stir
- Slow cooker mode on high for 4 hours or low for 8 hours
- Once cooked stir in the cream
- Add freshly chopped parsley to serve

SPEEDY VEGETABLE RISOTTO

This is an unbelievably quick, easy and tasty recipe! This a perfect quick lunch idea and if I make too much I simply save it for the next day. Risotto is one of my favourite things to eat when I am lucky enough to be in Italy and I have spent hours making risotto in the past but now I don't have to. You can add any leftover cooked chicken or prawns to this recipe.

All you need:

1 onion finely chopped
3 spring onions, chopped
Handful of mushrooms, chopped

vegetable stock 600ml
Salt and pepper
300g Risotto/ Arborio rice

1 garlic clove, finely chopped
Parmesan grated to serve

Method:

- Spray bowl with oil
- Add all chopped and peeled veg and the rice
- Make the stock and pour in, ensure the veg and rice is coved
- Pressure cook on high for 7 mins
- Add salt and pepper and grated parmesan to serve

HONEY GLAZED GAMMON

I love this at Christmas time! But who am I kidding, this is my staple to go to meals at any time. It is easy and adaptable and can go with anything. Pineapple, baked beans, egg, gravy, salad, vegetables, in a sandwich, with a cheese platter, chips... the list goes on. You can enjoy this hot or cold so it's great if you have any leftovers (I never have any leftovers with this!) it's the kind of food you keep going back to at a buffet until it's all gone. When I do have friends and family over at home for a buffet, this never fails to please everyone.

All you need:

Gammon joint 750g
Vegetable stock
2 Bay leaves
3 cloves of garlic
2 teaspoons of Oregano
Honey (I find squeezy honey the best)

Method:

- Place the gammon joint into the bowl
- Add the made up stock
- Add the bay leaves, roughly chopped garlic and oregano (add any other herbs you fancy)
- Pressure cook for 30 mins
- Quick release and carefully remove the gammon and removed the stock
- With a sharp knife score lines in the gammon joint and pour the honey over the gammon
- Add the gammon back in the ninja bowl and Air crisp for 12 minutes

PORK LEG (WITH CRACKLING)

Who doesn't love crackling? It can be a hard one to get right but the ninja makes it easy and delicious!

All you need:

Pork leg 1kg
Salt
vegetable stock

Method:

- Place the pork in the bowl with 300ml of vegetable stock and pressure cook for 20 mins on high
- Carefully remove the pork and remove the stock (can be used for gravy) leave the prok to stand for around 10 mins and pat dry with a tea towel
- Salt the rind of the pork then place back in the bowl and roast for 10 mins at 190
- Crisp fry for a further 10 mins (lower the time and keep checking if a smaller joint)

DONER KEBAB

Yes you read that right! You can make your own doner kebab at home in less than an hour. Serve with salad in pitta for a scrumptious treat.

All you need:

- 500g lamb mince
- 1 egg
- 2 teaspoons garlic powder
- 1 teaspoon black pepper
- 1 teaspoon salt
- 1 teaspoon oregano
- 1 teaspoon paprika
- 1 teaspoon chilli powder
- spray oil

Method:

- Whisk the egg
- Add all ingredients to a bowl (not your ninja bowl) and mix together really well with a few sprays of the oil
- Roll the mince mix into a loaf/large sausage shape firmly to ensure it doesn't fall apart, then wrap it in tin foil tightly no air bubbles so the water doesn't get in
- Add approx 3 cups of water and Pressure cook for 30 mins on high using the rack
- Remove foil and Air Crisp for 5 mins at 180c
- Use a potato peeler to create the kebab shop strips!

PASTA BOLOGNESE

This is the perfect one pot dish to make after a hard day's work, it's full of flavour and kids love it. Serve on its own, with salad, homemade chips or garlic bread.

All you need:

250g Beef mince
1 Onion, chopped
100g Mushrooms
2 Cloves of garlic, chopped and peeled

2 Tins of chopped tomatoes
Red pepper
350 ml Beef stock
200g dry pasta

1 teaspoon tomato puree
½ teaspoon mixed herbs
Spray oil

Method:

- Spray the bowl with oil and set to sauté, add the onion then the garlic (you can skip this part and just add n all the ingredients, for low fat mince 5% i put it all in together)
- Add the mixed herbs and mince to brown
- Once mince is brown but not fully cooked add all the other ingredients and stir
- Turn off saute and add the lid to pressure cook (ensure the lid is set to seal). Pressure cook for 8 mins on high
- Quick release for 5 mins

RICE PUDDING

My parents favourite is this creamy rice pudding for a warming dessert.

All you need:

200g pudding rice, rinsed in water

700ml of whole milk

75g castor sugar

50g Butter unsalted

For flavour can add Jam, chocolate, nutmeg, cinnamon for serving

Method:

- Add all ingredients to bowl and stir well (don't overfill)
- Pressure cook for 20 mins on Medium
- Quick release but leave in for 10 mins to thicken

FLUFFY WHITE RICE

Create a perfect fluffy white rice with this easy recipe.

All you need:

White rice
Cold water

Method:

- To keep it simple, for a cup of rice i add a cup of water and then a dash more water
- Pressure cook on high for 2 mins and leave to natural release for 10 mins (the rice is still cooking)
- Switch to Quick release for the remainder

SAUSAGE ROLLS

Perfect sausage rolls for a picnic at the park, you can also buy vegetarian sausages for a meat free alternative.

All you need:

Sausages/sausage meat shop bought/ ready made puff pastry

1 Egg for glaze splash of milk

Method:

- Unroll the pastry and use a knife to cut down the middle length ways
- Remove the skin from the sausages and place in the middle of each pastry length
- Mix the milk and egg yolk and brush down the side of the pastry and roll the pastry to make a sausage roll, use the mix to seal and slice to desired length
- Place in the ninja and set to bake for 15 mins at 190 until golden

SRIRACHA & HONEY SALMON

This is beautiful with stir fried vegetables (set Ninja to saute mode and stir fry) and fluffy white rice.

All you need:

Salmon fillet(s)
1 teaspoon of soy sauce
1 teaspoon of garlic paste
1 teaspoon of honey
1 teaspoon of sriracha sauce
Lime juice

Method:

- Mix the soy sauce, lime and garlic together and brush over the fillet
- Air crisp for 11 mins
- Mix the sriracha and honey to make a glaze and brush onto the salon, air crisp for a further 2/3 mins depending on the size of the fillet

TANDOORI DRUMSTICKS

For extra tastiness I marinate my chicken for a few hours or overnight if I can and find the best way of doing this is putting the mix and chicken in a freezer bag in the fridge overnight. If you haven't got the time to do that, it is still fabulous. If you prefer boneless chicken, use fillets instead.

All you need:

- Chicken legs (4)
- 1 teaspoon of salt
- 1 teaspoon of garlic & ginger paste (the world food aisle in supermarkets)
- 2 tablespoons of lemon juice
- 1 small pot of plain yogurt
- 1 teaspoon of garam masala
- 1 teaspoon of ground cumin
- 1 teaspoon chilli powder
- 2 teaspoon of tandoori powder
- spray oil

Method:

- Spray the oil and Sauté on low the spices and stir for 1 minute
- Turn off the heat and add yogurt, lemon juice, garlic & ginger paste and salt
- Mix in the chicken and transfer to a freezer bag to marinate for a few hours/overnight or pressure cook for 10 mins and then roast for 14 mins

TOMATO RISOTTO

This is a super easy risotto and I use this recipe while weaning my baby (leaving out the salt and pepper). You don't have to use sugar snap peas, you can really adapt this to use any veg that is going a little sad in the fridge or frozen peas, I use cherry tomatoes but any tomatoes chopped up would work. I sometimes serve it alongside a grilled chicken breast or a cod fillet.

All you need:

100g of risotto rice
390g Italian chopped tomatoes
sugar snap peas, chopped in half/thirds
1 onion, diced

a handful of cherry tomatoes, quartered
1 teaspoon oregano
1 clove of garlic
1 teaspoon of basil

Cheddar cheese, grated to serve
Fresh basil to serve (optional)
Spray oil
salt & pepper

Method:

- Spray bowl with oil
- Add in all the ingredients (apart from the cheese)
- Set to pressure cook for 8 mins
- Quick release and served with grated cheddar, salt and pepper to season (leave out if using for toddler

CHICKEN WINGS

You can buy chicken wings from most supermarkets and butchers at a really reasonable price. I think they are a perfect snack for watching football/rugby/cricket. There are tons of flavourings you can use for wings and you can prep and marinate the day before and store in the fridge overnight. Some of my favourites are Chinese, tandoori, jerk, bbq, garlic and herb, garlic and honey, lemon and garlic.

All you need:

Chicken Wings
Squeezy Honey
Dash of Soy Sauce
4 Cloves of Garlic,
crushed/minced
Oil Spray
Salt and Pepper

Method:

- Place the chicken wings in a bowl
- Add a big squeeze of honey, the garlic, splash of soy sauce and spray of oil and give mix it all up
- Place them in the Ninja bowl, depending on how many youve got you may have to do 2 batches because these on not be piled on top of each other for even cooking
- Air Crisp at 200c for 10-12 mins and turn over as required

KRISPY KALE

This is a great substitute to have instead crispy seaweed and a beautiful side to a home cooked Chinese or just as a tasty snack. You can put this in an airtight bag/container and it will last a few days (if there's any left).

All you need:

Bag of kale, big stalks chopped off
Spray oil
1 teaspoon of Chinese 5 spice

Method:

- In a bowl spray the kale with oil and sprinkle in around 1 teaspoon of Chinese 5 spice
- Air crisp for 8 mins

BISCOFF BROWNIES

This is a crowd pleaser! Absolutely scrumptious and so easy to make.

All you need:

210g Unsalted Butter
215g Dark Chocolate chopped
3 Eggs

275g Caster Sugar
150g Plain Flour
40g Biscoff Biscuits
(broken in uneven pieces)

75g Biscoff Spread/ Caramel spread
2-3 tbsp Caramel/Salted Caramel

Method:

- Preheat to 150c
- Spray a disposable foil container (20cm) with oil (like what you get in a takeaway, also great to use when cooking veg separately at the same time)
- Melt the chocolate and butter together (i do this is a bowl over a pan of water)
- Once slightly cooled, add the eggs and sugar and whisk in for 3 – 5 minutes
- Fold in the flour.
- Fold in the biscoff biscuits (try not to eat them) and pour into the foil container
- Add blobs of biscoff spread on top of the brownie batter and swirl in with a cocktail stick
- Set to Bake for 30 – 35 minutes
- Remove from the unit and drizzle over caramel (you can get this in squeezy bottles) and add crumbled Biscoff

CHEESE SCONES

I love eating these while they are still warm! Ideal for picnics and afternoon teas at home.

All you need:

125g cheddar , grated
225g self-raising flour
1 tsp baking powder
1 tsp mustard powder
Pinch of salt
50g Butter, cold, cut into cubes
7 tbsp milk

Method:

- Mix flour, baking powder, mustard powder and salt together
- Add butter, cheese and milk and knead together
- Use a cutter to make scone shape and brush with milk and top with cheese
- Place on greaseproof paper and select Bake for 12-15 minutes

PASTA ARRABIATA

This is a super simple pasta dish that can quickly and easily feed the full family. You can use any pasta you have in the cupboard, add in any veg you like (i like to add grated courgette, any sad looking tomatoes etc) and you can stir in some cream cheese at the end to make it creamy. I add any cheese that needs using up to be honest i either grate it on top to serve or add mozzarella at the end in the bowl and let it melt in. I like to mop up the sauce with some garlic bread.

All you need:

1 Red chilli. chopped
3 cloves of, grated
1 Red onion, diced
1tsp Dried Italian herbs
190ml Vegetable stock

1 x 400g Tinned tomatoes
2 tbsp Tomato puree
15-20g Fresh mixed herbs
or fresh basil (shredded)
Spray oil

Method:

- Start by selecting saute on high. Leave to heat up for a few minutes then add your spray oil, red onion, garlic, and dried Italian Herbs. Stir frequently until the onions have softened (about 2-3 minutes)
- Add the remaining ingredients to the cooking pot (pasta, stock etc) , leave out the cheese and fresh basil. Stir together then secure the pressure lid and lock in place. Set the valve to the seal position.
- Select pressure cook on high for 4 minutes. Let the programme run and allow the pressure to natural release for 3 minutes before quick releasing the pressure by turning the valve to vent and then remove lid
- Remove the lid and stir in the remaining ingredients until fully incorporated then serve immediately.

MULLED WINE

I love having this festive treat on the go when people come over because they can just help themselves and it brings a wonderful aroma to the kitchen and it's super easy but looks like you've gone to a lot of effect. I also don't believe you need to wait for Christmas to enjoy this, it's perfect after a chilly walk. Enjoy!

All you need:

750ml bottle of red wine	4 cloves	4 teaspoons caster sugar
1 large cinnamon stick	2 strips of lemon zest (use	Dehydrated orange slices
2 star anise	a veg peeler)	(optional)

Method:

- Pressure cook on high for 1 minute
- Quick release and set to 'KEEP WARM', ready to enjoy

FLAPJACKS

I take these flapjacks on outings for a filling snack and swap the syrup for honey and top with melted chocolate.

All you need:

110g Unrefined Demerara Sugar

170g Unsalted Butter

55g Golden Syrup

225G Porridge Oats

Method:

- Melt the butter. Add the syrup and sugar and mix together on low heat
- Remove from heat and add the oats and mix well
- Use grease proof paper and spread the mixture in a tin
- Bake setting for 20 mins at 170c

GREEN THAI CURRY

This yummy green thai curry is so good for a perfect night in.I steam shop bought dumplings for a starter and have a side of thai crackers & sweet chilli sauce for dipping. My kind of heaven.

All you need:

- 4 tbsp Thai green curry paste
- 400g Diced chicken breast
- 1 tin (400ml) coconut milk
- 200ml hot chicken stock
- 1 tbsp fish sauce
- 1 Red pepper, sliced
- 200g Mangetout
- 250g Mushrooms
- 1 Teaspoon brown sugar

Method:

- Select saute on high. Add the oil and curry paste and cook for 1 minute, stirring regularly
- Add the chicken, coconut milk, chicken stock, fish sauce and brown sugar and mix well. Turn off the heat
- Assemble the pressure lid, making sure the pressure release valve is in the seal position
- Pressure cook on high for 5 mins
- When pressure cooking is complete, allow pressure to natural release for 2 minutes. After 2 minutes, quick release the remaining pressure by turning the pressure release valve to the VENT position
- Carefully remove the lid when the unit has finished releasing pressure. Select saute and cook on high
- Add the mushrooms, red pepper and mangetout and cook for 4 minutes until the vegetables have softened but still retain a little crunch

HOT CHOCOLATE

Like most of the recipes this can be done in the slow cooker also, it probably depends on how quick you want it.

All you need:

1 Litre Milk
300ml Double Cream
200g Dark Chocolate, chopped
100g Milk Chocolate, chopped

To Serve:

Mini Marshmallows
Grated chocolate
Squirty Cream

Method:

- Put all the ingredients in the bowl and stir
- Pressure cook on low for 5 minutes. Once cooked, quick release the pressure. Stir and Serve with mini marshmallows, squirty cream and grated chocolate

TIP: Alternatively slow cook for 2 hours and stir halfway through

CLEGGYS CHILLI

Even the fussiest eaters enjoy this chilli, I do sometimes add in grated courgette and carrots because no one ever notices and I like to get my 5 a day. I personally leave out the kidney beans but add them if you like them. I serve with a dollop of cream cheese, grated cheddar & fluffy white rice and air crisp tortillas on the side.

All you need:

500g Minced Beef	2 Teaspoon Ground Cumin	1 red chilli
2 Medium Onions, diced		400g Tin of Chopped Tomatoes
250g Mushroom, chopped	2 Teaspoon Ground Coriander	
1 Red Pepper		3 Tablespoons Tomato Puree
3 Garlic Cloves, finely chopped	1 Teaspoon Oregano	
	1 Bay Leaf	1 Tablespoon of Beef Gravy Granules
2 Teaspoons of Chilli Powder	Salt & Pepper	
	450ml Beef stock	Spray oil

To serve:

Fresh Coriander
Grated cheddar
Cream Cheese

Method:

- Turn sautee on high and spray with oil
- Add the beef, season with salt & pepper and brown
- Add the chopped garlic, onions, red chilli, pepper and mushrooms and stir
- Add the rest of the ingredients and give it a good , turn off saute
- Put on the pressure lid and pressure cook for 25 mins on high

AIR CRISP TORTILLAS

I serve these with Cleggys Chilli and they are literally done by the time ive served out the chilli. Other days I add passata, more cheddar or mozzarella and some ham and make a pizza out of it for a quick lunch, either way, they are a hit.

All you need:

Tortilla Wrap
Handful of grated Cheddar
Sprinkle of Garlic Salt

Method:

- Place wrap in the ninja bowl and sprinkle with the grated cheddar and garlic salt
- Air crisp on 200 for 3 mins

HALLOUMI OMELETTE

You can adapt this recipe to add and take out anything you like.

All you need:

6 Eggs
Spray oil
25g Halloumi, cut into cubes
1 Onion, diced
Handful of Cherry Tomatoes, halved
Pinch of Salt

Method:

- Crack open and beat the eggs in a separate bowl, add a pinch of salt
- Put Saute on high and add spray oil and onions, lighty stir for 2 mins, turn off heat
- Add the beaten eggs, halloumi and tomatoes
- Air crisp for 5 mins

SPANISH CHICKEN

I make this when my parents come and babysit for me, I just put it all in and tell them to help themselves when it's ready. The bonus is I can have any leftovers.

All you need:

Spray oil
Boneless Chicken Thighs (4)
1 Onion, diced
150g Mushrooms

1 Yellow Pepper
1 Courgette, chopped
100g Chorizo, sliced
400g Chopped Tomatoes

1 Teaspoon tomato puree
1 Teaspoon Oregano
Chicken stock 190ml

To Serve: Fresh Parsley

Method:

- Set the ninja to Saute and spray with oil and had the chicken thighs to brown, don't worry, these don't have to be cooked through at this stage. Once chicken is browned, turn off saute
- Add the rest of the ingredients to the chicken and stir
- Add the pressure lid and pressure cook for 30mins

CHICKPEA CURRY

For this easy curry you probably have the ingredients in already making it a staple meal in my house and great to the freeze. I served this with white rice.

All you need:

- Spray Oil
- 1 Onion, diced
- 1 Red Chilli
- 2 Cloves of Garlic
- 3cm of Grated Ginger
- 1 Teaspoon Ground Coriander
- 2 Teaspoons Ground Cumin
- 1 Tablespoon Garam Masala
- 2 Tablespoon Tomato Puree
- 2 Cans of Chickpeas
- 400g can of Chopped Tomatoes
- Handful of Spinach
- Fresh Coriander

Method:

- Using sauté setting on your ninja, set the temperature to medium/low and spray with oil
- Add onions, garlic, chilli, ground coriander, cumin, garam masala and tomato puree and stir for a 2 mins
- Drain and add the chickpeas and chopped tomatoes
- Put the pressure lid on pressure cook for 3 minutes
- Once the 3 minutes have finished, leave the vent closed for a further 5 minutes to allow the temperature to drop naturally
- Take lid off and mix in chopped fresh coriander and spinach until wilted

FISH PIE

This warming fish pie is a lovely comfort food for any season and I enjoy it with asparagus, long stem broccoli and peas. You can swap white wine for fish stock and cod for salmon.

All you need:

1kg potatoes, peeled, cut into cubes	50g butter	150g Broccoli, Chopped small
250ml water	1 Onion, Chopped	500g cod fillets, cut into cubes
50g butter	50g plain flour	
70ml milk	100ml white wine (can swap for fish stock)	200g peeled cooked prawns
Pinch of Salt	350ml milk	2 tbsp fresh parsley
Salt and Pepper	150ml single cream	50g grated Gruyere cheese

Method:

- Place potatoes and water into the pot. Assemble pressure lid, making sure the pressure release valve is in the seal position
- Pressure cook on high for 7 minutes
- When pressure cooking is complete, quick release the pressure by moving the pressure release valve to the vent position. Carefully remove lid when unit has finished releasing pressure
- Drain potatoes if necessary, transfer to a separate bowl and mash with butter, milk, salt & pepper and cover to keep warm and keep to one side for now
- Select saute and set to 4 (medium high) and heat for 2 mins
- Add the butter to melt then the onion and sauté until soft for 5mins, stirring occasionally. Add flour and sauté for 30 secs/minute. Gradually stir in the wine, milk and cream. Keep stirring to ensure it is not lumpy, cook for 2mins

- Add the broccoli, select saute and set to 3 (medium). Cook for a few minutes, then set to 2 (low-medium) stir in cod, prawns, parsley, season to taste and simmer for a few more minutes. Top with the mashed potatoes, and sprinkle grated cheese over the top
- Close the crisping lid; select bake for 20 mins at 170c

CAMEMBERT DIPPERS

These taste amazing dipped in chilli jam or any of your favourite dips. I like to serve this alongside a crudite platter with celery, carrots, cucumber, mini bell peppers, asparagus and cherry tomatoes. They also go lovely with a cheese board and a glass of red wine.

All you you need:

1 x 200g pack Camembert (or Brie) block, cut into 10-12 wedges
50g plain flour
1 egg, beaten
60g Breadcrumbs
Salt & Pepper

Method:

- Place the flour on one plate, beaten egg in a bowl and the breadcrumbs mixed with salt & pepper in another bowl
- For each wedge of cheese, roll it in the flour to coat, then dip in the egg, then roll in the breadcrumbs to coat and put to one side and continue to do thest rest
- Once complete, put them carefully in the basket and air crips at 200C for 12 minutes

STRAWBERRY JAM

This recipe can be adapted to most seasonal fruit and this strawberry jam is beautiful on toast, jam tarts and with porridge. If storing away, remember to sterilise your jars to prevent any mould developing. Once you start making your own, you'll never buy jam again! You can do the same for Rhubarb, raspberries etc, whatever is in season at the time. Great little gifts for neighbours and friend too.

All you need:

900g whole or diced strawberries
450g Jam sugar

Method:

- Add the fruit and sugar to the pot and stir
- Assemble the pressure lid, making sure the pressure release valve is in the seal position. Pressure cook on high for 6 mins
- When pressure cooking is complete, allow pressure to natural release for 10 minutes. After 10 minutes, quick release remaining pressure by moving the pressure release valve to the vent position. Carefully remove lid when unit has finished releasing pressure
- Stir well, and mash fruit if desired, you can do with a potato masher

PIZZA SWIRLS

These are handy little snacks and great for the weekend because they can be easily reheated and you can add any leftover meat and veg you have. I like to have them with a salad or air crisps with a few dips on the side. So quick and easy annnnd everyone loves pizza, right?

All you need:

1 ready to use pizza dough roll - supermarket chilled section (or you can use home made)	Sprinkle of Garlic Salt 170g mozzarella - grated Packet of sliced pepperoni 200g tomato passata	1 tsp oregano 1 tsp basil Spray oil Salt and pepper

Method:

- In a bowl mix the tomato passata, garlic salt, oregano, basil, salt and pepper
- Set temperature to 200°C for 10 mins to preheat
- Roll out pizza dough and evenly spread tomato sauce onto it
- Cover the dough with ½ of the mozzarella, then top with pepperoni and sprinkle again with remaining cheese
- Roll dough with its toppings so it looks like a rolled carpet, lightly brush the edge with water to make sure it sticks well and close the roll
- Cut the pizza roll into 2cm wide slices (wheel shaped swirls)
- Once unit has beeped to signify it has preheated, line crisper basket with baking paper and pop in the pizza swirls
- Add crisper basket to the unit and select bake at 200°C for 10 mins

SWEET POTATO FRIES

Guilt free fries that basically go with anything.

All you need:

750g Sweet Potatoes, cut into chips/fries
Spray Oil
Salt & Pepper

Method:

- Cut potatoes into evenly sized chips and add to the basket of your Ninja Foodi
- Spray with oil and spread evenly, season with salt & pepper
- Select Air crisp at temp 180c for 15 mins, shake the basket every 5 minutes

CAULIFLOWER CHEESE

The perfect compliment to a sunday roast!

All you need:

1 medium head of cauliflower, cut into florets
250ml water
500ml whole or semi skimmed milk

50g unsalted butter, cut into small cubes
50g Plain Flour
1 Teaspoon dried mustard powder

Salt & Pepper
100g Cheddar, grated

Method:

- Place cauliflower florets and water in the pot
- Pressure cook on low for 1 minute
- When pressure cooking is complete, quick release the pressure by moving the pressure valve to the vent position. Carefully remove lid when unit has finished releasing pressure
- Use a colander to drain and wipe out the pot
- Select saute and set to 4 (medium-high)
- Add milk, butter and flour to pot and using a silicone whisk, whisk together continuously until sauce starts to thicken, this may take several minutes. Turn down the heat to 2 (low medium)
- Add the mustard powder, seasoning and half the cheese
- Stir in the drained cauliflower and sprinkle over the remaining cheese
- Close crisping lid and air crisp at temp 200c for 7 mins

FRUIT CAKE

Tea and cake, yes please.

All you need:

255g Butter (room temp)
600g of dried fruit (soaked overnight in rum or brandy if you like)
225g Plain Flour

2 teaspoons of baking powder
150g Caster Sugar
4 Eggs

Method:

- Whisk the butter and sugar until light and fluffy
- Add the eggs one at a time
- Add flour, baking powder and the fruit and mix
- Add to a baking tin then place the baking tin in the ninja bowl
- Bake for 55mins at 160c

CHEESE TOASTIE

The perfect snack, a delicious toastie in your foodi (which goes perfectly with a bowl of homemade soup!)

All you need:

Bread
Butter
Cheese

Method:

- Butter you bread on both sides (outer sides too)
- Make a cheese sandwich (you can add extra fillings- tomatoes, ham etc)
- Air crisp at 190c for 7 mins

FRIED CHICKEN

You will never want takeaway chicken again, this tastes like it's from the chicken shop, but better.

All you need:

2 Tablespoons salt
1.5 tablespoons black peppercorn
1 tablespoon garlic granules
1 tablespoon Rosemary
1/2 tablespoon dried basil

1/2 tablespoon paprika
1/2 tablespoon dried oregano
1/2 tablespoon yellow mustard seeds1 teaspoon Thyme
teaspoon tarragon

350g plain flour
2 chicken breasts cut into 5 strips each
2 eggs beaten in a bowl
Spray Oil

Method:

- Place all spices and herbs into a mixer and blend until find grind
- Add flour and continue mixing
- Pour 1/3 of the flour onto a plate
- Coat chicken strips in egg and then flour. Then put them in egg and then flour again.
- Place chicken in air fryer and drizzle oil for crispy coating. Cook for five minutes on each side

POTATO SKINS

Never throw out potato peelings again! Serve with your favourite dips.

All you need:

The Peelings of Potato
Spray Oil
Salt & Pepper

Method:

- Place potato skins in ninja bowl
- Spray with oil and season with salt & pepper
- Aircrip for 18 mins

CHICKEN AND CHORIZO PAELLA

This spanish classic is super quick and you can add other seafood and meat or leave out and make it veggie or vegan. I personally love to add in prawns and squid.

All you need:

Spray oil	100g chorizo, chopped	150g frozen peas
1 onion, diced	1/2 Teaspoon, smoked paprika	300g paella rice
1 garlic clove, chopped		700ml hot vegetable stock
300g chicken thighs, chopped	1 Teaspoon chopped rosemary	75ml white wine
4 Large Tomatoes, diced	1 Red Pepper, diced	

Method:

- Select saute and press high, allow the pot to heat up for 3 minutes
- Add the oil and onions, mix with a wooden spoon and cook for 2-3 minutes.
- Add the garlic, tomato, chicken thighs and chorizo and cook for 3 minutes until the chicken is cooked
- Add the remainder of the ingredients – paprika, rosemary, red pepper, frozen peas, rice, stock and wine and sir
- Pressure cook on high for 7 minutes
- When pressure cooking is complete, allow the pressure to natural release for 2 minutes. After 2 minutes, quick release the pressure by turning the pressure release valve to the vent position. Carefully remove lid when unit has finished releasing pressure

ROAST VEG TRAY BAKE

This is lovely alongside a roast or can be had as a meal on its own. Add any seasonal veg and fresh herbs you may have. You can also add cheese.

All you need:

2 Onions	2 Potatos, cubed	2 Garlic cloves, crushed
2 Courgettes	2 Peppers	Salt and Pepper
Handful of Brussel Sprouts	4 Portobello Mushrooms	Mixed Herbs, sprinkle
	Spray oil	

Method:

- Select roast, set temperature to 180c, and set time to 20 mins and preheat for 2 mins
- Spray the bowl with oil and add the vegetables, herbs and garlic. Season with salt and pepper and give it all a stir
- Cook on roast at 180c for 20 mins
- Stir after 20 mins and continue to cook for a further 10mins

STUFFED MUSHROOMS

This is a gorgeous starter if you are having a date night and is a satisfying served with a fresh salad.

All you need:

Portobello Mushrooms (4)
Mozzarella (any melty cheese can be used), grated
Handful of Cherry Tomatoes, halved
Spring Onions, Chopped
2 Cloves of Garlic, crushed
Spray oil

Method:

- Remove the stalk from the mushroom and spray with oil
- On each mushroom sprinkle on cheese, then add on each of the veg then sprinkle more cheese on top of the veg
- Place in the ninja bowl and bake for 12 mins for 190c

DUMPLING SOUP

This is sooo yummy and quick! You can add dried noodles to make this into ramen or add any leftover chicken/pork. My absolute favourite.

All you need:

Ready made veg gyoza/dumpling (frozen aisle in the supermarket)
1 Veg stock cube
1 Chicken stock cube
1 Red chilli, chopped
1 Bell Pepper, chopped
4 Spring onions, chopped
2 Handfuls of baby spinach
Splash of Soy Sauce
1 Teaspoon chinese 5 spice

Method:

- Add all ingredients to the ninja bowl with 1 litre of water
- Pressure cook 2 mins
- Natural release 1 min
- Done!

Printed in Great Britain
by Amazon